Mindset Moments

GRADES

Handwriting
Practice

 Newmark Learning • 145 Huguenot Street • New Rochelle, NY • 10801

© Newmark Learning, LLC. All rights reserved. Teachers may photocopy the reproducible pages in this book for classroom use.
No other part of this publication may be reproduced or transmitted in whole or in part in any form or by any means, electronic or
mechanical, including photocopy, recording, or any information storage or retrieval system, without permission in writing from the publisher.
Printed in Guangzhou, China. 4401/1117/CA21701357

ISBN 978-1-4788-6131-7
For ordering information, call Toll-Free 1-877-279-8388 or visit our website at www.newmarklearning.com.

Table of Contents

Introduction 3

Uppercase Letter Formation Practice 5

Lowercase Letter Formation Practice 6

Practice Sheets

1. Always Keep Learning 7
2. Be the Best 8
3. Change Your Mindset 9
4. Don't Give Up 10
5. Everyone Makes Mistakes 11
6. Finish What You Start 12
7. Give It Your All 13
8. Hard Work Pays Off 14
9. If I Keep Trying 15
10. Just Stay Calm 16
11. Keep Going 17
12. Learn a New Way 18
13. My Mistakes 19
14. Never Give Up 20
15. One Try 21
16. Practice Makes Perfect 22
17. Quality Work 23
18. Reach for the Stars! 24
19. Share Your Solutions 25
20. Train Your Brain 26

21. Use Mistakes 27
22. Victory Is When I Try 28
23. We Learn 29
24. X Out Poor Habits 30
25. You Can Do It 31
26. Zoom In 32
27. Learning Can Be Fun! 33
28. Have I Done My Best? 34
29. It Is Okay to Not Know 35
30. Take Time 36
31. Give It Your Best 37
32. Review Your Work 38
33. I Like to Be Challenged 39
34. Try to Explain 40
35. If You're Stuck 41
36. Just Don't Quit 42
37. How Will You Solve It? 43
38. I Am Not Afraid 44
39. It's Not Okay 45
40. I Can Learn to Print 46

How to Make a Growth Mindset Moment Booklet 47

Blank Practice Sheet 48

Introduction

Welcome to *Grades K–1: Mindset Moments Handwriting Practice*—the perfect resource to help kids practice their handwriting skills using growth mindset sentences.

Many young learners struggle when they begin to write. Learning to form letters with lines, circles, and a few strokes, and then writing legible words and sentences can be challenging. However, with enough practice, perseverance and a growth mindset, students can master this skill. This book is full of meaningful sentences for kids to practice handwriting while forming a positive growth mindset.

The 40 practice sheets in this book were developed to give children handwriting practice and opportunities to hone their fine-motor skills using growth mindset sentences such as: "Always keep learning," and "My mistakes help me grow."

How to Use This Book

You can use this book in a variety of ways. Here are a few ideas:

- Photocopy and distribute the Uppercase and Lowercase Letter Formation Practice pages for each child to keep at their desk. Students can reference these pages as they write their sentences.

- Before distributing the practice sheets to your students, write the growth mindset sentence on the board and model standard letter formation.

- Generate rich discussions about growth mindset traits by introducing each sentence to the class. You may start by sharing what the sentence means and why it is meaningful.

- Challenge students to complete a practice sheet when they arrive in the morning.

- Invite partners or small groups to share and discuss their written sentences.

- Laminate the practice sheets and keep them in a writing center for students to complete independently with a dry erase pen. You can also keep laminated copies of the letter formation pages for children to reference as they write.

- Send home a practice sheet each night for students to complete independently or with the help of a parent, guardian, or older sibling.

- Provide copies of the blank sheet on page 48 for additional practice.

How to Use the Practice Sheets

Each practice sheet, designed to help students develop their writing skills, is comprised of four parts:

1 Trace the words. In this section, students trace a growth mindset word with the aid of dotted letters. The initial words on the first 26 pages are in alphabetical order to offer children practice with all upper- and lowercase letters. Note: You can have students complete the practice sheets in any order you choose, especially if they are having difficulty with a particular letter or group of letters.

2 Practice writing this word.
Next, children write a key word from the growth mindset sentence without the aid of dotted letters. They can practice writing the word as many times as space allows.

3 Trace the sentence. In this section, children write the growth mindset sentence on the write-on lines provided. Encourage children to analyze their writing and focus on four areas: letter formation, sizing of letters, line alignment, and spacing between letters and words.

Optional: After children write their sentences, they can use the pages to create their own Growth Mindset Moment book. For instructions on how to make the booklet, see page 47.

Uppercase Letter Formation Practice

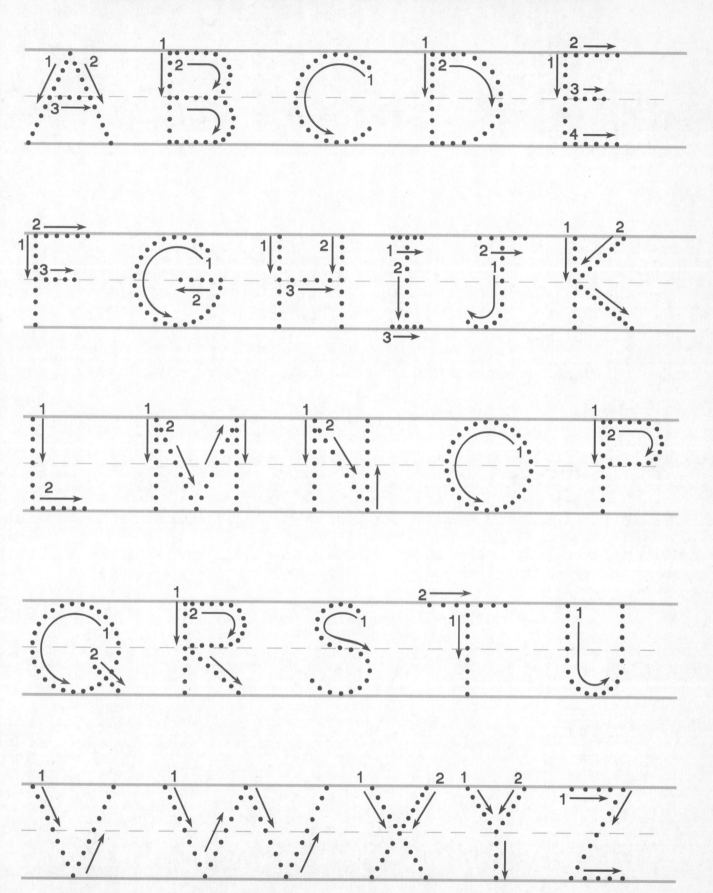

Lowercase Letter Formation Practice

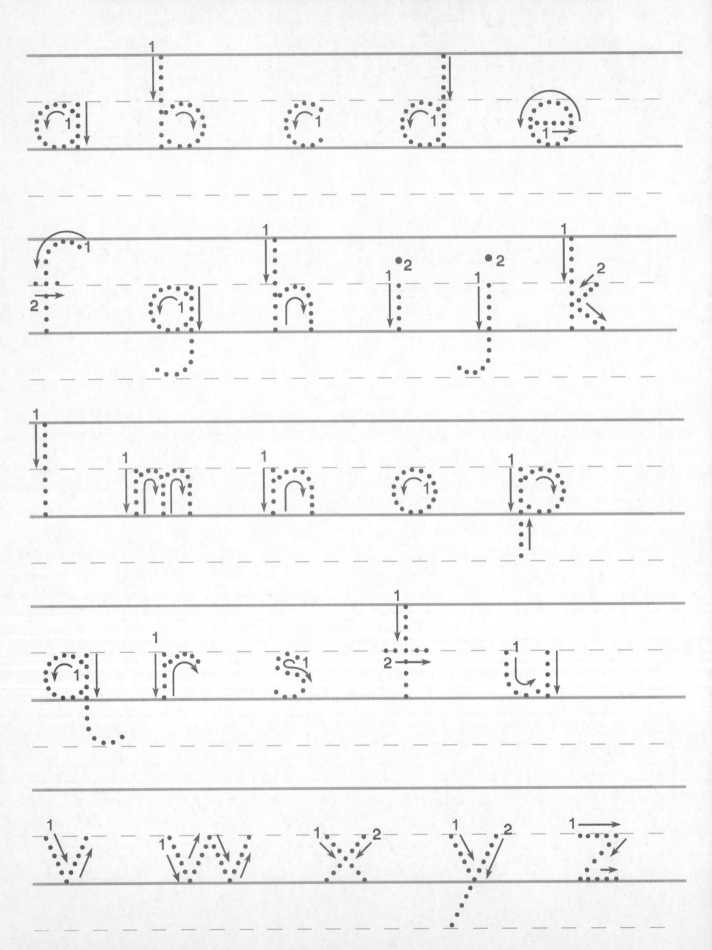

Name _____

Always Keep Learning

1 Trace the words.

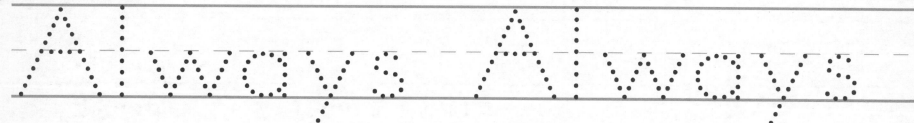

2 Practice writing this word.

3 Trace the sentence.

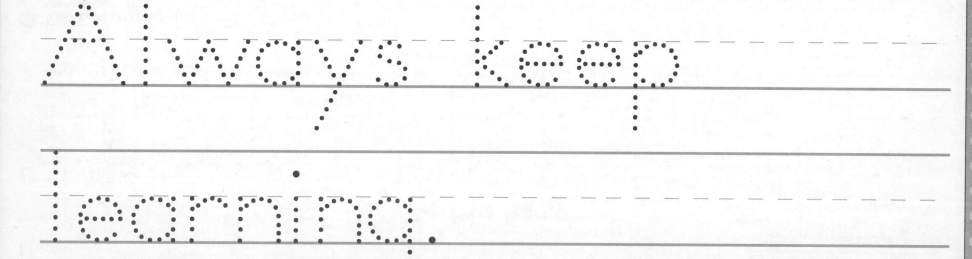

Name _____

Be the Best

1 Trace the words.

Be   Be   Be   Be

2 Practice writing this word.

3 Trace the sentence.

Be the best by

trying harder.

Name _____

Change Your Mindset

1 Trace the words.

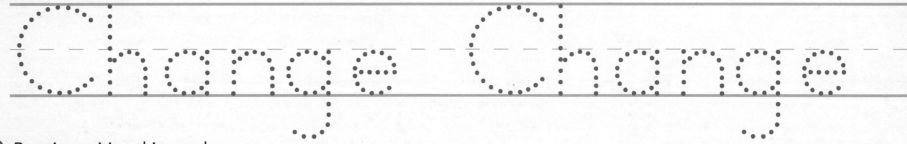

2 Practice writing this word.

3 Trace the sentence.

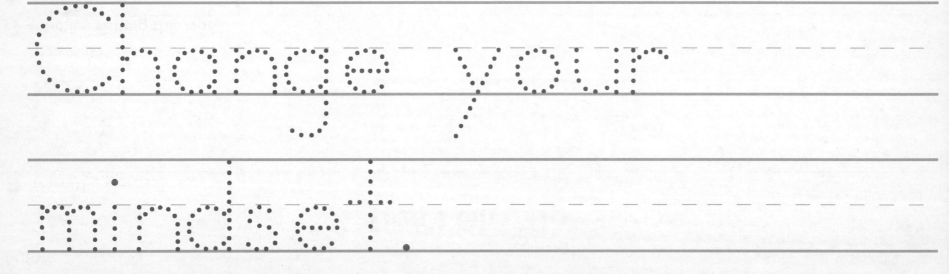

Grades K-1:Mindset Moments Handwriting Practice © Newmark Learning, LLC • page 10

Name _____

Don't Give Up

1 Trace the words.

Don't Don't

2 Practice writing this word.

Don't

3 Trace the sentence.

Don't give up.

You can do it!

Grades K-1: Mindset Moments Handwriting Practice © Newmark Learning, LLC • page 11

Everyone Makes Mistakes

1 Trace the words.

Everyone

2 Practice writing this word.

Everyone

3 Trace the sentence.

Everyone makes mistakes.

Name _____

Finish What You Start

1 Trace the words.

Finish Finish

2 Practice writing this word.

Finish

3 Trace the sentence.

Finish what you start. Always!

Grades K–1: Mindset Moments Handwriting Practice © Newmark Learning, LLC • page 13

Give It Your All

1 Trace the words.

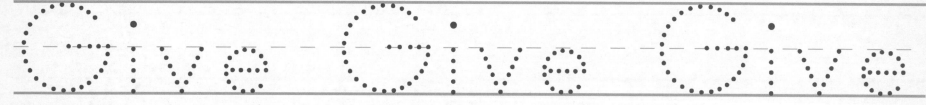

2 Practice writing this word.

3 Trace the sentence.

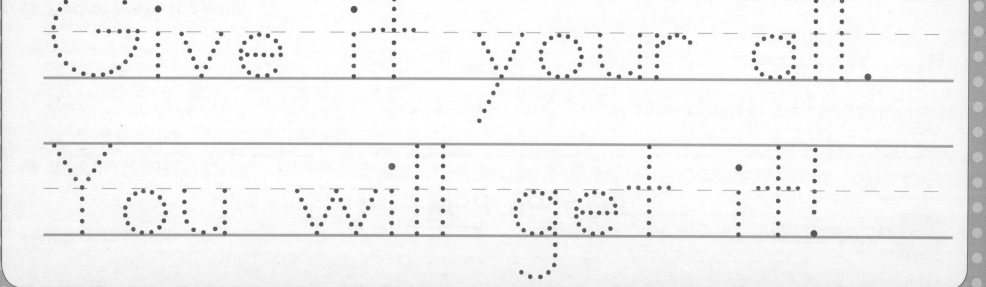

Hard Work Pays Off

❶ Trace the words.

Hard Hard Hard

❷ Practice writing this word.

Hard

❸ Trace the sentence.

Hard work

pays off.

Name _____

If I Keep Trying

1 Trace the words.

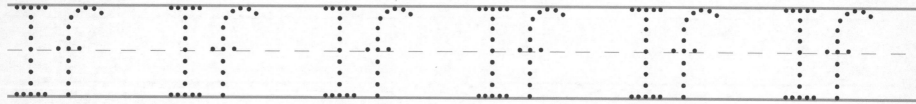

2 Practice writing this word.

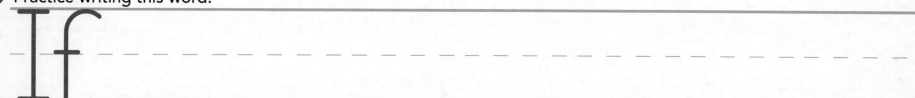

3 Trace the sentence.

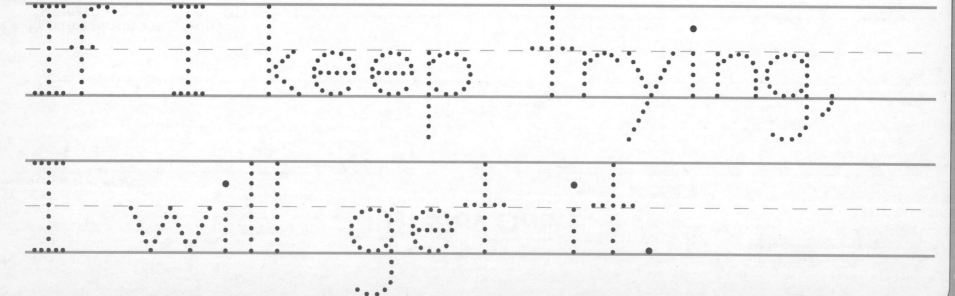

Name _____

Just Stay Calm

❶ Trace the words.

Just   Just   Just

❷ Practice writing this word.

Just

❸ Trace the sentence.

Just stay calm
and focus.

Name _____

Keep Going

1 Trace the words.

Keep Keep Keep

2 Practice writing this word.

Keep

3 Trace the sentence.

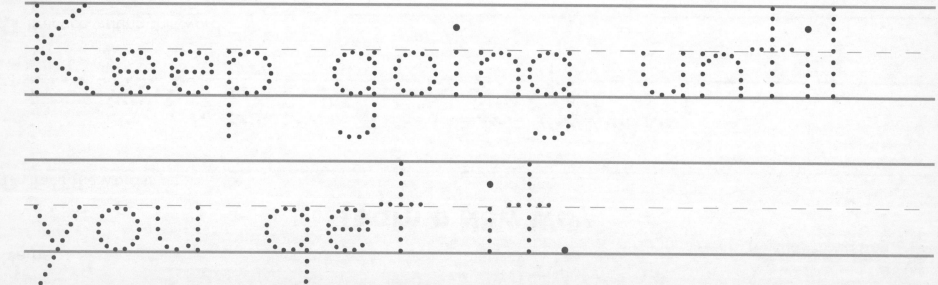

Keep going until

you get it.

Grades K–1: Mindset Moments Handwriting Practice © Newmark Learning, LLC • page 17

Learn a New Way

1 Trace the words.

Learn Learn

2 Practice writing this word.

Learn

3 Trace the sentence.

Learn a new

way to solve it.

My Mistakes

❶ Trace the words.

My My My My My

❷ Practice writing this word.

My

❸ Trace the sentence.

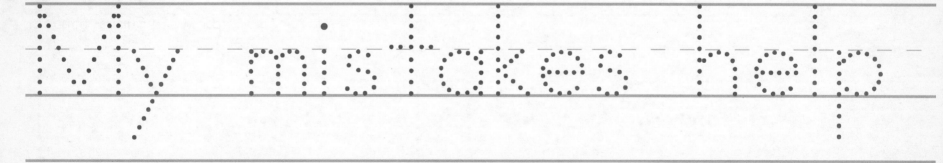

My mistakes help

me grow.

Grades K-1 Mindset Moments Handwriting Practice © Newmark Learning, LLC • page 20

Never Give Up

❶ Trace the words.

Never Never

❷ Practice writing this word.

Never

❸ Trace the sentence.

Never, ever, ever

give up!

Name _____

One Try

1 Trace the words.

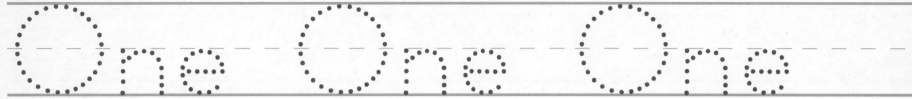

One One One

2 Practice writing this word.

One

3 Trace the sentence.

One try may not

be enough.

Name _____

Practice Makes Perfect

1 Trace the words.

Practice

2 Practice writing this word.

Practice

3 Trace the sentence.

Practice makes

perfect.

Quality Work

Grades K–1: Mindset Moments Handwriting Practice © Newmark Learning, LLC • page 23

❶ Trace the words.

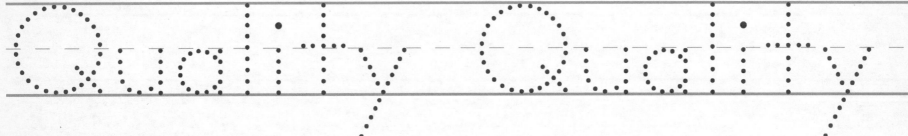

❷ Practice writing this word.

❸ Trace the sentence.

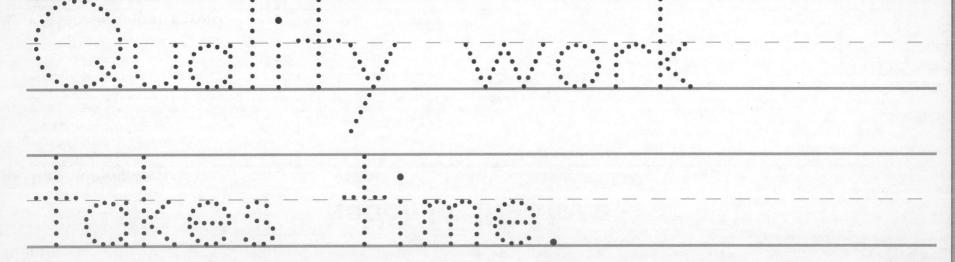

Reach for the Stars!

1 Trace the words.

Reach Reach

2 Practice writing this word.

Reach

3 Trace the sentence.

Reach for

the stars!

Share Your Solutions

1 Trace the words.

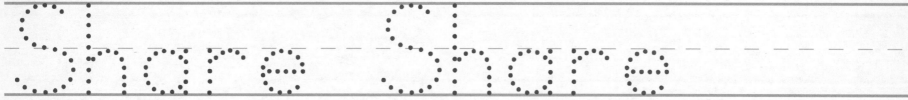

2 Practice writing this word.

3 Trace the sentence.

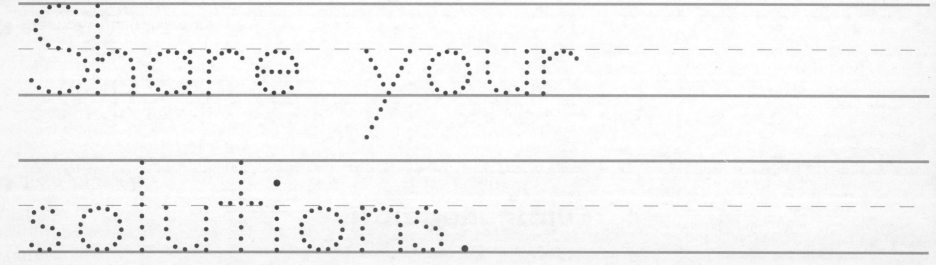

Name _____

Train Your Brain

1 Trace the words.

Train Train

2 Practice writing this word.

Train

3 Trace the sentence.

Train your brain

to do it.

Use Mistakes

1 Trace the words.

Use Use Use

2 Practice writing this word.

Use

3 Trace the sentence.

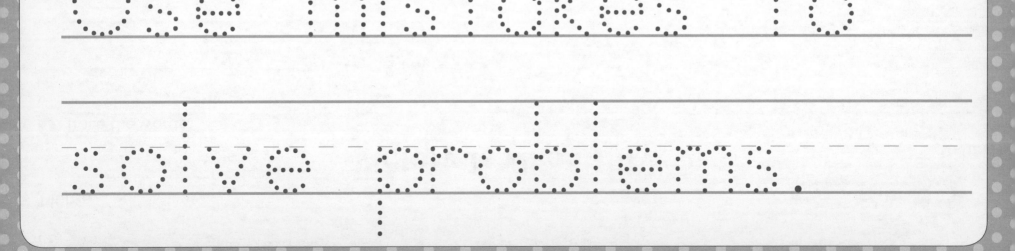

Use mistakes to

solve problems.

Grades K–1: Mindset Moments Handwriting Practice © Newmark Learning, LLC • page 27

Name _____

Victory Is When I Try

1 Trace the words.

Victory Victory

2 Practice writing this word.

Victory

3 Trace the sentence.

Victory is when
I try my best.

Grades K-1 Mindset Moments Handwriting Practice © Newmark Learning, LLC • page 29

Name _____

We Learn

❶ Trace the words.

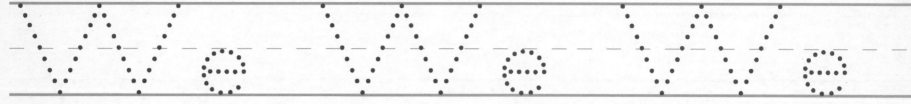

We We We

❷ Practice writing this word.

We

❸ Trace the sentence.

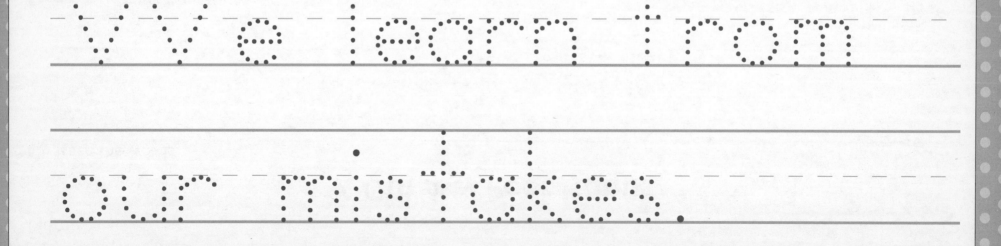

We learn from our mistakes.

Name _____

X Out Any Poor Habits

1 Trace the words.

X out X out

2 Practice writing this phrase.

X out

3 Trace the sentence.

X out any poor

habits.

You Can Do It

❶ Trace the words.

You   You   You

❷ Practice writing this word.

❸ Trace the sentence.

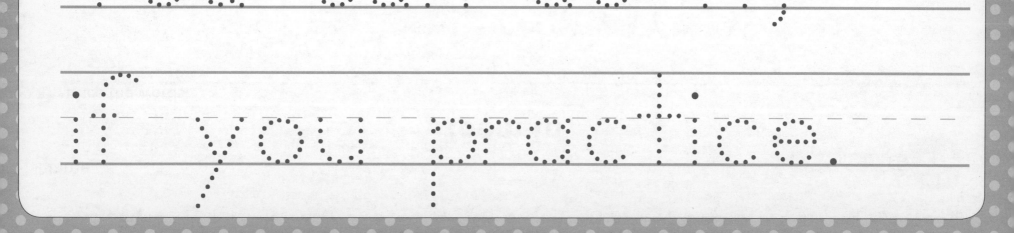
You can do it,

if you practice.

Grades K–1: Mindset Moments Handwriting Practice © Newmark Learning, LLC • page 31

Name _____

Zoom In

1 Trace the words.

Zoom   Zoom

2 Practice writing this word.

Zoom

3 Trace the sentence.

Zoom in on

your strengths.

Name _____

Learning Can Be Fun!

1 Trace the words.

2 Practice writing this word.

Learning

3 Trace the sentence.

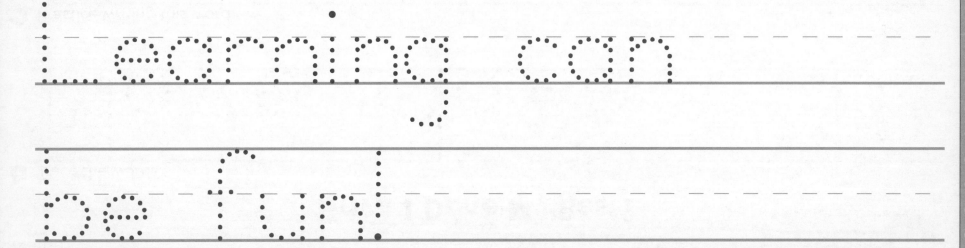

Name _____

Have I Done My Best?

❶ Trace the words.

Have Have

❷ Practice writing this word.

Have

❸ Trace the sentence.

Have I done

my best?

Name _____

It Is Okay to Not Know

1 Trace the words.

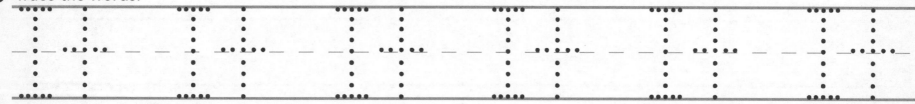

2 Practice writing this word.

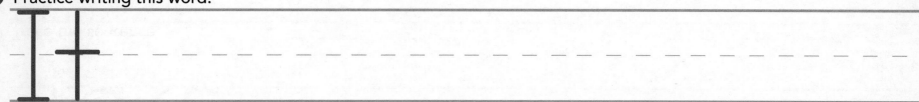

3 Trace the sentence.

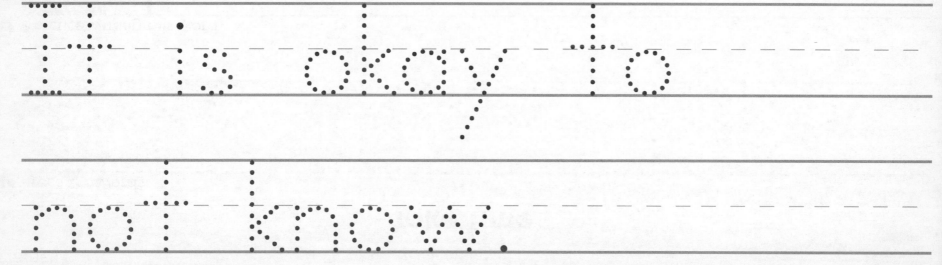

Take Time

1 Trace the words.

Take   Take   Take

2 Practice writing this word.

Take

3 Trace the sentence.

Take time to

do it right.

Grades K–1 Mindset Moments Handwriting Practice © Newmark Learning, LLC • page 37

Give It Your Best

❶ Trace the words.

❷ Practice writing this word.

your

❸ Trace the sentence.

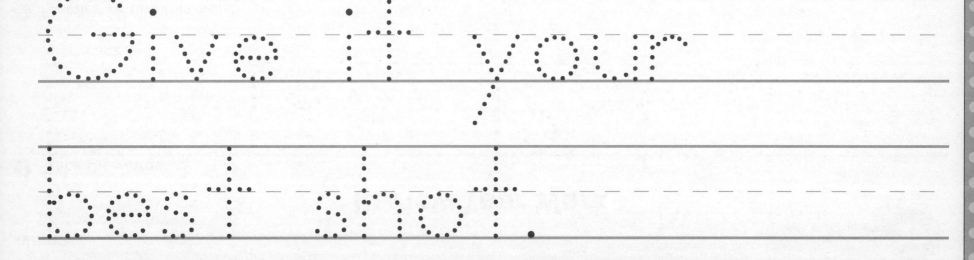

Review Your Work

1 Trace the words.

Review Review

2 Practice writing this word.

Review

3 Trace the sentence.

Review your

work.

I Like to Be Challenged

1 Trace the words.

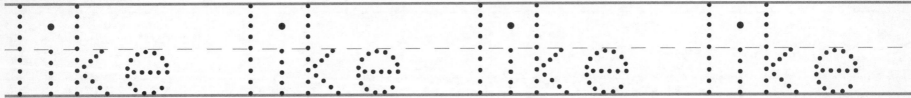

like like like like

2 Practice writing this word.

like

3 Trace the sentence.

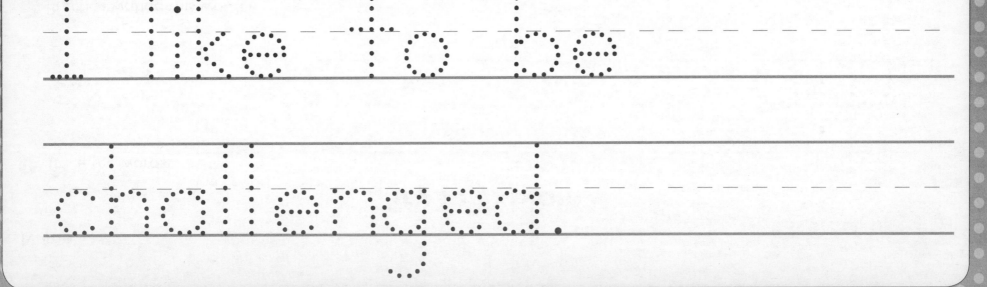

I like to be challenged.

Name _____

Try to Explain

❶ Trace the words.

explain   explain

❷ Practice writing this word.

explain

❸ Trace the sentence.

Try to explain

your thinking.

If You're Stuck

1 Trace the words.

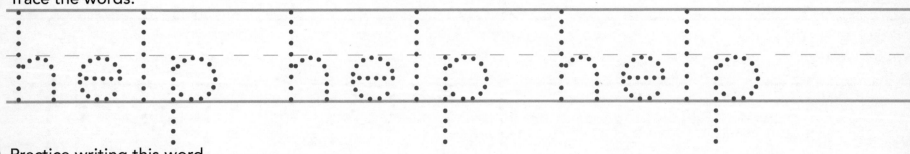

help help help

2 Practice writing this word.

help

3 Trace the sentence.

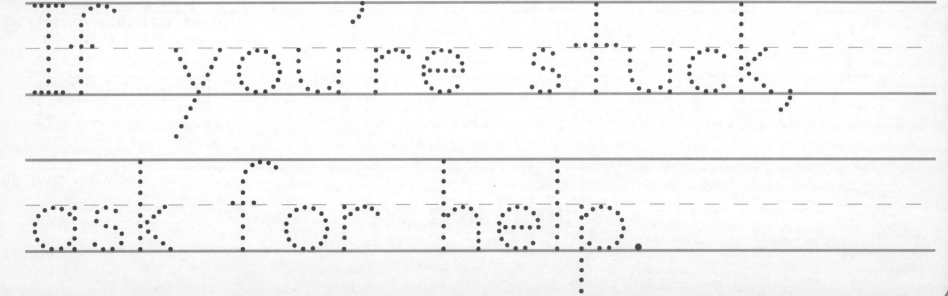

If you're stuck, ask for help.

Grades K-1 Mindset Moments Handwriting Practice © Newmark Learning, LLC • page 42

Name _____

Just Don't Quit

1 Trace the words.

quit   quit   quit

2 Practice writing this word.

quit

3 Trace the sentence.

Just don't

quit, ever!

How Will You Solve It?

❶ Trace the words.

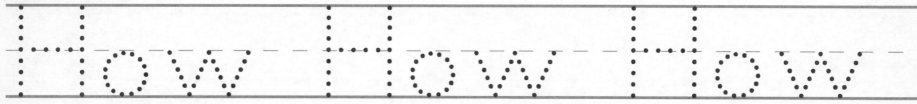

Ｈｏｗ Ｈｏｗ Ｈｏｗ

❷ Practice writing this word.

Ｈｏｗ

❸ Trace the sentence.

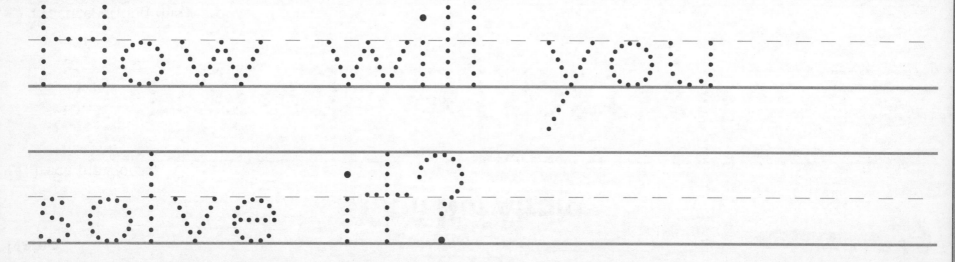

How will you

solve it?

Grades K–1: Mindset Moments Handwriting Practice © Newmark Learning, LLC • page 43

I Am Not Afraid

1 Trace the words.

afraid afraid

2 Practice writing this word.

afraid

3 Trace the sentence.

I am not afraid

of hard work.

It's Not Okay

❶ Trace the words.

okay okay okay

❷ Practice writing this word.

okay

❸ Trace the sentence.

It's not okay to
not try.

Name _____

I Can Learn to Print

1 Trace the words.

print   print   print

2 Practice writing this word.

print

3 Trace the sentence.

I can learn to

print well.

How to Make a Growth Mindset Moment Booklet

1 After students finish tracing their sentences, ask them to cut the pages above the "Trace the sentence" section, discarding the top portion.

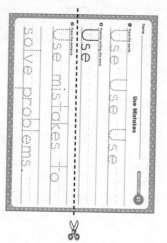

2 Make photocopies of the booklet cover at the right of this page and distribute them. Ask children to place the booklet cover on top of the pages, stacked in any order they choose. Optional: They can color the booklet cover and the interior pages.

3 Staple the booklet pages along the left-hand side.

My Growth Mindset Moment Book

Written by

PRACTICE SHEET